The owner of this book is:

Name

_____

Telephone

_____

Date Purchased

_____

Other Information

_____

_____

_____

_____

_____

_____

SIMPLY EV'REET
Learning Biblical Hebrew Through Studying the Names of God
by Nelda A. Billups

Copyright © 2014 Nelda A. Billups

All rights reserved. No part of this publication may be used or reproduced in any manner whatsoever without written permission from the author, except in the case of brief quotations embodied in critical articles or reviews. For more information contact the author.

Download MP3 Simply Ev'reet   www.simplyevreet.com

Cover and text design by Lucy Iloenyosi, NeatWorks, Inc.

About the Author

Nelda A. Billups, M. Ed., is a retired public school Lead Educator and Curriculum Council Chair who is now a teacher of Biblical Hebrew. She also teaches ESOL and regularly welcomes immigrants to their new country during Naturalization Ceremonies.

LEARNING BIBLICAL HEBREW
Through Studying the Names of God

SIMPLY EV'REET

Nelda A. Billups

Table of Contents

Acknowledgements v

Author's Notes vi

To the Learner vi

SECTION I 1

Learning Biblical Hebrew Through Studying the Names of God

Order of Hebrew Alef Bet 2

Alef Bet Practice Chart 3

Vowels, Names and Sounds 4

About *Tanakh* Names 5

Torah, Prophets, Writings (English List) 6

Torah, Prophets, Writings (Ev'reet List) 8

Reflections 10

Genesis – II Chronicles 12

SECTION II 123

Sh-mah V-ah-hav-tah

SECTION III 127

God of Israel, The Jewish People, Land of Promise

SECTION IV 131

Ah-me-dah

SECTION V 135

Additional Names of God

SECTION VI 145

Concluding Reflections

Acknowledgements

This book is from and for the God of Abraham, Isaac and Jacob.

Ye shall not add unto the word which I command you, neither shall ye diminish ought from it, that ye may keep the commandments of the Lord your God which I command you.
Deuteronomy 4:2

Gather the people together, men and women and children, and thy stranger that is within thy gates, that they may hear, and that they may learn, and fear the Lord your God, and observe to do all the words of this Torah…
Deuteronomy 31:12

Many thanks to Rebitsen Rachel Wolf and Mrs. Phyllis Adler Blackburn for their invaluable observations regarding this Workbook Primer.

Many thanks to all who have made it possible for me to begin and continue my Hebrew Learning Path—to all listed and to all who prefer not to be listed.

Rabbi Michael R. Wolf
Rabbi Jean Eglinton
Mrs. Rachel Rachovitsky

Many thanks to Mrs. Heather Goodman for her creative artwork, Mrs. Nancy Shockey for editing the English, Mrs. Hope Wozniak for editing the Hebrew.

Simply Ev'reet CD - Shofar sound bite from the *Praise Awaits You* CD by Paul L. Rogers, copyright 1993. Used with permission.

Author's Notes

Tree of Life

The *Tanakh** is truly "…a Tree of Life…" (if) one takes hold of it. I am among those who have been able and privileged to do so.

This *Simply Ev'reet* Workbook and CD will be an amazing encouragement as you begin to read, write and understand Biblical Hebrew. These lessons will be your Hebrew foundation, the first "rung on the ladder." Finish this Workbook Primer and then use it as your foundational reference as you "keep stepping." There is so much more you can learn and apply. You will become more and more confident as your learning and understanding increases. This learning path will be a remarkable voyage.

Contents are my responsibility; please excuse errors and the liberties I have taken.

Included are some of the favorite Names and some that may be new to you. Add your favorites in the section *Additional Names of God.* Most of the Names are in the Male (M) gender, either Singular (S) or Plural (P); the few exceptions are noted as Feminine (F).

Often in Hebrew literature or other writings you will notice that the English translations may be written without vowels, as traditionally, the Hebrew language is written without vowels. I have chosen not to follow this practice because English speakers and writers use vowels in the written language. (God not G-d, Lord not L-rd) This is my preference.

My hope is that you will enjoy your Hebrew learning path as much as I am enjoying my Hebrew learning path. I also hope that your eyes and heart will be open to the Jewish people, their history, land and lifestyles.

**Tanakh*: Torah, Prophets, Writings*

To the Learner

Assuredly, this publication will give you an excellent fundamental, important foundation in Biblical Hebrew. This Workbook Primer is an easy introduction and is presented in an uncomplicated format. The many repetitions you will see are crucial when learning a new language.

Follow the instructions, listen often to the CD and complete the Workbook Primer--you will be creating your own Reference Source.

The learning ladder is ready for your ascent to higher and higher levels of Ev'reet wisdom. You will have the confidence to continue your Biblical Ev'reet (Biblical Hebrew) learning with further advanced study and/or Higher Education Classes.

Mazel Tov!

SECTION I

Learning Biblical Hebrew Through Studying the Names of God

Order of Hebrew Alef Bet
Record of Learning and Letter Practice Page

Write and practice the letters often as you learn them. After you have learned all letters, memorize them in the **following correct order** so that you can use reference materials as you advance your learning. (Note how the writing of transliteration names varies.)

Name	Hebrew Letter	Sound	Practice All Letters
Aleph/Alef	א	Silent	
Bet	ב	(B)lack	
Gimel/Gimmel	ג	(G)irl	
Dalet/Daled	ד	(D)oll	
Hey	ה	(H)ay	
Vav	ו	(V)ow	
Zayin/Zayeen	ז	(Z)ebra	
Chet	ח	(Kh)aki	
Tet	ט	(T)aught	
Yud/Yod	י	(Y)es /silent	
Kaf/Cuff *	כ ך	(K)it	
Lamed	ל	(L)ove	
Mem*	מ ם	(M)other	
Nun*	נ ן	(N)one	
Samech	ס	(S)un	
Ayin	ע	Silent	
Pay/Pey*	פ ף	(P)ayment	
Tsade/Tsadi*	צ ץ	nu(TS)	
Koof/Qof	ק	(K)eep	
Resh/Reysh	ר	(R)un	
Shin	ש	(SH)irt	
Tav/Tuf	ת	(T)ight	

* includes 5 Final Hebrew letters

Alef Bet Practice Chart

NAME and PRINT Each Letter. PRINT from Right to Left.

	ג		ב		א
	ו		ה		ד
	ט		ח		ז
	ך		כ		י
	ם		מ		ל
	ס		ן		נ
	ף		פ		ע
	ק		צ		צ
	ת		ש		ר

Vowels, Names and Sounds

VOWEL NAMES	SYMBOLS	SOUNDS	עִבְרִית
Qames/Qamets	ָX	ah as in b(ah)	קָמֵץ
Patah/Patach	ַX	ah as in b(ah)	פַּתַח
Hireq/Chireq	ִX	ee as in b(ee)	חִירֶק
Sere/Tsere	ֵX	eh as in mikv(eh)	צֵרִי
Segol	ֶX	eh as in mikv(eh)	סֶגוֹל
Holem/Cholem	ֹX	o as in (oh)	חוֹלָם
Holem/Cholem Vav	וֹ	o as in (oh)	חוֹלָם וָו
Qibbus/Qibbuts	ֻX	oo as in p(ooh)	קֻבֵּץ
Sureq/Shureq	וּ	oo as in p(ooh)	שׁוּרֶק
Hataf qames/Qamets	ֳX	o as in (oh)	חֲטָף קָמֵץ
Hataf patach	ֲX	ah as in b(ah)	חֲטָף פַּתַח
Hataf segol	ֱX	eh as in mikv(eh)	חֲטָף סֶגוֹל
Sere/Tsere Yud	ֵיX	a as in h(ay)	צֵרִי יוּד
Shva/Sheva	ְX	eh as in mikv(eh) OR can also be with no sound, Silent	שְׁוָא

Note: Xs are the letters (X) to indicate consonants

About Tanakh Names

The Name of God and His Titles or Attributes

People often speak of the "Names" of God to refer to the many titles God is given in Scriptures. Most of these titles reveal one or more of God's attributes. These are not technically God's "proper name" but rather a form of address that expresses who God is or how God is acting, at a particular time in the Scriptures. In this Workbook Primer we will be studying some of the Titles of God used in the *Tanakh* (Hebrew Bible).

In contrast, God does reveal to Moses in Exodus 3:14-15 what could be considered something like His "proper Name." This Name is designated by the four Hebrew letters: yud, hey, vav, hey, often translated "I Am Who I Am." These four letters together form what is commonly known as the Tetragrammaton (a Greek word meaning four letters).

Over time, the correct pronunciation of this Name was lost. For reasons of respect, and to avoid using the Name of God in vain, Jewish tradition forbids the pronunciation of this Name and avoids writing this Name except in sacred texts (like the Torah scroll) that will not ever become trash. When Jewish people read this Name they say LORD or Adonai which is LORD in Hebrew. In books other than the sacred scroll, even in prayer books, the Name of God is written in Hebrew יְיָ **(yud yud).** Consequently, when the Tetragrammaton is found in a Title of God in this Workbook Primer, you will see the יְיָ **(yud yud)** which should be read as "Adonai." The translation is LORD and in a few instances the translation will be GOD. Note in either translation, it is written in all capital letters.

Torah, Prophets, Writings (English List)

Add page numbers as you learn each Name

Torah, Prophets, Writings (*Tanakh*)	Titles/Names of God	List Page
Torah		
Genesis 1:1	God	
Exodus 3:14	I Am Who I Am	
Exodus 15:26	LORD Who heals you	
Exodus 17:15	LORD my Banner	
Leviticus 4:22	LORD his God	
Numbers 6:2	(to the/for the) LORD	
Deuteronomy 6:4	LORD our God	
Prophets		
Joshua 3:10	Living God	
Judges 6:24	LORD of Peace	
I Samuel 2:3	LORD God of Knowledge	
I Samuel 15:29	Strength of Israel	
II Samuel 22:29	LORD my Light	
I Kings 18:36	LORD God of Abraham Isaac and Israel	
II Kings 17:26-27	God of the Earth	
Isaiah 9:5	Wonderful	
Isaiah 9:5	Counselor	
Isaiah 9:5	Mighty God	
Isaiah 9:5	Eternal Father	
Isaiah 9:5	Prince of Peace	
Jeremiah 10:7	King of the Nations	
Jeremiah 23:6	LORD our Righteousness	
Ezekiel 47:23	Lord GOD	
Ezekiel 48:35	LORD is There	
Hosea 2:18	LORD my Husband	

Joel 3:16	LORD is a Refuge and Strength	
Amos 3:13	Lord GOD God of the Hosts (Armies)	
Obadiah 1:15	LORD	
Jonah 1:9	LORD God of the Heavens	
Micah 4:2	God of Jacob	
Micah 7:8	LORD is Light to me /LORD (is my) Light	
Nahum 3:5	LORD of Hosts (Armies)	
Habakkuk 1:12	LORD my God, my Holy One	
Zephaniah 3:17	LORD your God (FS)	
Haggai 1:14	Their God	
Zechariah 3:8	Branch	
Malachi 2:17	God of Judgment	
Writings		
Psalms 9:3	Most High	
Proverbs 2:17	(F) Her God	
Job 5:17	Almighty	
Job 19:25	My Redeemer	
Song of Songs 8:14	(Lord) my Beloved	
Ruth 1:16	and Your God, My God (FS)	
Ruth 2:12	LORD God of Israel	
Lamentations 3:41	(To/for) God	
Ecclesiastes 12:1	Your Creator	
Esther	No Name is written	
Daniel 9:4	Lord the Great and Dreadful God	
Ezra 7:27	LORD God of our Fathers	
Nehemiah 9:17	God of Forgiveness	
I Chronicles 22:12	LORD your God (MS/MP)	
I Chronicles 22:18	LORD your God (MP)	
II Chronicles 15:1	Spirit of God	

Torah, Prophets, Writings (Ev'reet List)

Add page numbers as you learn each Name

Torah, Prophets, Writings		עַמּוּד
Torah	**תּוֹרָה**	
Genesis 1:1	אֱלֹהִים	
Exodus 3:14	אֶהְיֶה אֲשֶׁר אֶהְיֶה	
Exodus 15:26	יְיָ רֹפְאֶךָ	
Exodus 17:15	יְיָ נִסִּי	
Leviticus 4:22	יְיָ אֱלֹהָיו	
Numbers 6:2	לַיְיָ	
Deuteronomy 6:4	יְיָ אֱלֹהֵינוּ	
Prophets	**נְבִיאִים**	
Joshua 3:10	אֵל חַי	
Judges 6:24	יְיָ שָׁלוֹם	
I Samuel 2:3	יְיָ אֵל דֵּעוֹת	
I Samuel 15:29	נֵצַח יִשְׂרָאֵל	
II Samuel 22:29	יְיָ נֵירִי	
I Kings 18:36	יְיָ אֱלֹהֵי אַבְרָהָם יִצְחָק וְיִשְׂרָאֵל	
II Kings 17:26-27	אֱלֹהֵי הָאָרֶץ	
Isaiah 9:5	פֶּלֶא	
Isaiah 9:5	יוֹעֵץ	
Isaiah 9:5	אֵל גִּבּוֹר	
Isaiah 9:5	אֲבִי־עַד	
Isaiah 9:5	שַׂר־שָׁלוֹם	
Jeremiah 10:7	מֶלֶךְ הַגּוֹיִם	
Jeremiah 23:6	יְיָ צִדְקֵנוּ	
Ezekiel 47:23	יְיָ אֲדֹנָי	
Ezekiel 48:35	יְיָ שָׁמָּה	
Hosea 2:18	יְיָ אִישִׁי	

Joel 3:16	יְיָ מַחֲסֶה וּמָעוֹז	
Amos 3:13	אֲדֹנָי יְיָ אֱלֹהֵי הַצְּבָאוֹת	
Obadiah 1:15	יְיָ	
Jonah 1:9	יְיָ אֱלֹהֵי הַשָּׁמַיִם	
Micah 4:2	אֱלֹהֵי יַעֲקֹב	
Micah 7:8	יְיָ אוֹר לִי	
Nahum 3:5	יְיָ צְבָאוֹת	
Habakkuk 1:12	יְיָ אֱלֹהֵי קְדֹשִׁי	
Zephaniah 3:17 (F)	יְיָ אֱלֹהַיִךְ	
Haggai 1:14	אֱלֹהֵיהֶם	
Zechariah 3:8	צֶמַח	
Malachi 2:17	אֱלֹהֵי הַמִּשְׁפָּט	
Writings	**כְּתוּבִים**	
Psalms 9:3	עֶלְיוֹן	
Proverbs 2:17 (F)	אֱלֹהֶיהָ	
Job 5:17	שַׁדַּי	
Job 19:25	גֹּאֲלִי	
Song of Songs	(אֲדֹנָי) דּוֹדִי	
Ruth 1:16 (F)	אֱלֹהַיִךְ אֱלֹהָי	
Ruth 2:12	יְיָ אֱלֹהֵי יִשְׂרָאֵל	
Lamentations 3:41	אֶל-(אֵל)	
Ecclesiastes 12:1	בּוֹרְאֶיךָ	
Esther	No Name is written	
Daniel 9:4	אֲדֹנָי הָאֵל הַגָּדוֹל וְהַנּוֹרָא	
Ezra 7:27	יְיָ אֱלֹהֵי אֲבוֹתֵינוּ	
Nehemiah 9:17	אֱלוֹהַּ סְלִיחוֹת	
I Chronicles 22:12 (MS/MP)	יְיָ אֱלֹהֶיךָ	
I Chronicles 22:18 (MP)	יְיָ אֱלֹהֵיכֶם	
II Chronicles 15:1	אֱלֹהִים רוּחַ	

Reflections

At this point in your study, consider taking time to reflect and think about why you have chosen to complete this *Simply Ev'reet Workbook Primer*. What goals did you set? Have they been met? Have your studies so far affected you in any way? What other comments do you have? Date and list your reflections before continuing your studies.

Date: _____

_____

_____

_____

_____

_____

_____

_____

_____

_____

_____

_____

_____

_____

Eh-lo-heem .... אֱלֹהִים

Chapter/Verse: Genesis 1:1
Hebrew: אֱלֹהִים
Transliteration: Eh-lo-heem
Translation: God

Practice writing, saying Eh-lo-heem.

NAME	SOUND		LETTER
Aleph	Silent		א
	Eh		אֱ
Lamed	l		ל
Cholem	lo		לֹ
Hey	h		ה
Yud	y		י
Final Mem	m		ם
	heem		הִים

Eh-lo-heem .... אֱלֹהִים

12 | SIMPLY EV'REET

Eh-lo-heem .... אֱלֹהִים

Chapter/Verse: Genesis 1:1
Hebrew: אֱלֹהִים
Transliteration: Eh-lo-heem
Translation: God

This Chapter: Practice writing in Hebrew and saying aloud the Hebrew Title often. You can also make notes, list questions to research, etc.

God .... אֱלֹהִים

_____

_____

_____

_____

_____

_____

_____

_____

_____

_____

Eh-yeh Ah-sher Eh-yeh .... אֶהְיֶה אֲשֶׁר אֶהְיֶה

Chapter/Verse: Exodus 3:14
Hebrew: אֶהְיֶה אֲשֶׁר אֶהְיֶה
Transliteration: Eh-yeh Ah-sher Eh-yeh
Translation: I Am Who I Am

Practice writing, saying Eh-yeh Ah-sher Eh-yeh.

NAME	SOUND		LETTER
Aleph	Silent		א
	Eh		אֶ
Hey	h		ה
	heh		הֶ
Yud	y		י
	yeh		יֶ
Aleph	Silent		א
	Ah		אֲ
Shin	sh		שׁ
Resh	r		ר
	sher		שֶׁר
Aleph	Silent		א
	Eh		אֶ
Hey	h		ה
	heh		הֶ
Yud	y		י
	yeh		יֶ

Eh-yeh Ah-sher Eh-yeh .... אֶהְיֶה אֲשֶׁר אֶהְיֶה

Eh-yeh Ah-sher Eh-yeh .... אֶהְיֶה אֲשֶׁר אֶהְיֶה

Chapter/Verse: Exodus 3:14
Hebrew: אֶהְיֶה אֲשֶׁר אֶהְיֶה
Transliteration: Eh-yeh Ah-sher Eh-yeh
Translation: I Am Who I Am

This Chapter: Practice writing in Hebrew and saying aloud the Hebrew Title often. You can also make notes, list questions to research, etc.

I Am Who I Am .... אֶהְיֶה אֲשֶׁר אֶהְיֶה

Ah-doe-nigh Rof-eh-kha .... יְיָ רֹפְאֶךָ

Chapter/Verse: Exodus 15:26
Hebrew: יְיָ רֹפְאֶךָ
Transliteration: Ah-doe-nigh Rof-eh-kha
Translation: LORD Who heals you

Practice writing, saying Ah-doe-nigh Rof-eh-kha.

NAME	SOUND		LETTER
Yud	y		י
	Ah-doe-nigh		יְיָ
Resh	r		ר
Cholem	ro		רֹ
Fey	f		פ
	Rof		רֹפְ
Aleph	Silent		א
	eh		אֶ
Final Kaf	k		ך
	kha		ךָ

Ah-doe-nigh Rof-eh-kha .... יְיָ רֹפְאֶךָ

Ah-doe-nigh Rof-eh-kha .... יְיָ רֹפְאֶךָ

Chapter/Verse: Exodus 15:26
Hebrew: יְיָ רֹפְאֶךָ
Transliteration: Ah-doe-nigh Rof-eh-kha
Translation: LORD Who heals you

This Chapter: Practice writing in Hebrew and saying aloud the Hebrew Title often. You can also make notes, list questions to research, etc.

LORD Who heals you .... יְיָ רֹפְאֶךָ

_____

_____

_____

_____

_____

_____

_____

_____

_____

_____

_____

SIMPLY EV'REET | 17

Ah-doe-nigh Nee-see .... יְיָ נִסִּי

Chapter/Verse: Exodus 17:15
Hebrew: יְיָ נִסִּי
Transliteration: Ah-doe-nigh Nee-see
Translation: LORD my Banner

Practice writing, saying Ah-doe-nigh Nee-see.

NAME	SOUND		LETTER
Yud	y		יְ
	Ah-doe-nigh		יְיָ
Nun	n		נ
	Nee		נִ
Samech	s		ס
	see		סִּי

Ah-doe-nigh Nee-see .... יְיָ נִסִּי

SIMPLY EV'REET

Ah-doe-nigh Nee-see .... יְיָ נִסִּי

Chapter/Verse: Exodus 17:15
Hebrew: יְיָ נִסִּי
Transliteration: Ah-doe-nigh Nee-see
Translation: LORD my Banner

This Chapter: Practice writing in Hebrew and saying aloud the Hebrew Title often. You can also make notes, list questions to research, etc.

LORD my Banner .... יְיָ נִסִּי

_____

_____

_____

_____

_____

_____

_____

_____

_____

_____

_____

_____

Ah-doe-nigh Eh-lo-hav .... יְיָ אֱלֹהָיו

Chapter/Verse: Leviticus 4:22
Hebrew: יְיָ אֱלֹהָיו
Transliteration: Ah-doe-nigh Eh-lo-hav
Translation: LORD his God

Practice writing, saying Ah-doe-nigh Eh-lo-hav.

NAME	SOUND		LETTER
Yud	y		יְ
	Ah-doe-nigh		יְיָ
Aleph	Silent		א
	Eh		אֶ
Lamed	l		ל
Cholem	lo		לֹ
Hey	h		ה
Yud	y		י
Vav	v		ו
	hav		הָיו

Ah-doe-nigh Eh-lo-hav .... יְיָ אֱלֹהָיו

Ah-doe-nigh Eh-lo-hav .... יְיָ אֱלֹהָיו

Chapter/Verse: Leviticus 4:22
Hebrew: יְיָ אֱלֹהָיו
Transliteration: Ah-doe-nigh Eh-lo-hav
Translation: LORD his God

This Chapter: Practice writing in Hebrew and saying aloud the Hebrew Title often. You can also make notes, list questions to research, etc.

LORD his God .... יְיָ אֱלֹהָיו

La-doe-nigh .... לַיְיָ

Chapter/Verse: Numbers 6:2
Hebrew: לַיְיָ
Transliteration: La-doe-nigh
Translation: To/For the LORD

Practice writing, saying La-doe-nigh.

NAME	SOUND		LETTER
Lamed	l		ל
	lah		לַ
Yud	y		י
	Ah-doe-nigh		יָיְ

La-doe-nigh .... לַיְיָ

La-doe-nigh .... לַיי

Chapter/Verse: Numbers 6:2
Hebrew: לַיי
Transliteration: La-doe-nigh
Translation: To/For the LORD

This Chapter: Practice writing in Hebrew and saying aloud the Hebrew Title often. You can also make notes, list questions to research, etc.

To/For the LORD .... לַיי

_____

_____

_____

_____

_____

_____

_____

_____

_____

_____

_____

Ah-doe-nigh Eh-lo-hey-new .... יְיָ אֱלֹהֵינוּ

Chapter/Verse: Deuteronomy 6:4
Hebrew: יְיָ אֱלֹהֵינוּ
Transliteration: Ah-doe-nigh Eh-lo-hey-new
Translation: LORD our God

Practice writing, saying Ah-doe-nigh Eh-lo-hey-new.

NAME	SOUND		LETTER
Yud	y		יְ
	Ah-doe-nigh		יְיָ
Aleph	Silent		א
	eh		אֱ
Lamed	l		ל
Cholem	lo		לֹ
Hey	h		ה
Yud	y		י
	hey		הֵי
Nun	n		נ
Shuruk	Vav		וּ
	new		נוּ

Ah-doe-nigh Eh-lo-hey-new .... יְיָ אֱלֹהֵינוּ

24 | SIMPLY EV'REET

Ah-doe-nigh Eh-lo-hey-new .... יְיָ אֱלֹהֵינוּ

Chapter/Verse: Deuteronomy 6:4
Hebrew: יְיָ אֱלֹהֵינוּ
Transliteration: Ah-doe-nigh Eh-lo-hey-new
Translation: LORD our God

This Chapter: Practice writing in Hebrew and saying aloud the Hebrew Title often. You can also make notes, list questions to research, etc.

LORD our God .... יְיָ אֱלֹהֵינוּ

_____

_____

_____

_____

_____

_____

_____

_____

_____

_____

El Khai .... אֵל חַי

Chapter/Verse: Joshua 3:10
Hebrew: אֵל חַי
Transliteration: El Khai
Translation: Living God

Practice writing, saying El Khai.

NAME	SOUND		LETTER
Aleph	Silent		א
	eh		אֶ
Lamed	l		ל
Chet	kh		ח
Yud	y		י
	khai		חַי

El Khai .... אֵל חַי

El Khai .... אֵל חַי

Chapter/Verse: Joshua 3:10
Hebrew: אֵל חַי
Transliteration: El Khai
Translation: Living God

This Chapter: Practice writing in Hebrew and saying aloud the Hebrew Title often. You can also make notes, list questions to research, etc.

Living God .... אֵל חַי

_____

_____

_____

_____

_____

_____

_____

_____

_____

_____

_____

Ah-doe-nigh Sha-lom............................יְיָ שָׁלוֹם

Chapter/Verse: Judges 6:24
Hebrew: יְיָ שָׁלוֹם
Transliteration: Ah-doe-nigh Sha-lom
Translation: LORD of Peace

Practice writing, saying Ah-doe-nigh Sha-lom.

NAME	SOUND		LETTER
Yud	y		יְ
	Ah-doe-nigh		יְיָ
Shin	sh		שׁ
	Sha		שָׁ
Lamed	l		ל
Vav	v		ו
Cholem Vav	oh		וֹ
Final Mem	m		ם
	lom		ל

Ah-doe-nigh Sha-lom............................יְיָ שָׁלוֹם

Ah-doe-nigh Sha-lom.................... יְיָ שָׁלוֹם

Chapter/Verse: Judges 6:24
Hebrew: יְיָ שָׁלוֹם
Transliteration: Ah-doe-nigh Sha-lom
Translation: LORD of Peace

This Chapter: Practice writing in Hebrew and saying aloud the Hebrew Title often. You can also make notes, list questions to research, etc.

LORD of Peace .... יְיָ שָׁלוֹם

_____

_____

_____

_____

_____

_____

_____

_____

_____

_____

_____

_____

Ah-doe-nigh El Deh-oat............ יְיָ אֵל דֵּעוֹת

Chapter/Verse: I Samuel 2:3
Hebrew: יְיָ אֵל דֵּעוֹת
Transliteration: Ah-doe-nigh El Deh-oat
Translation: LORD God of Knowledge

Practice writing, saying Ah-doe-nigh El Deh-oat.

NAME	SOUND		LETTER
Yud	y		י
	Ah-doe-nigh		יְיָ
Aleph	Silent		א
Lamed	l		ל
	El		אֵל
Dalet	d		ד
Ayin	Silent		ע
	Deh		דֵּע
Cholem Vav	oh		וֹ
Tav	t		ת
	oat		וֹת

Ah-doe-nigh El Deh-oat .... יְיָ אֵל דֵּעוֹת

30 | SIMPLY EV'REET

Ah-doe-nigh El Deh-oat .... יְיָ אֵל דֵּעוֹת

Chapter/Verse: I Samuel 2:3
Hebrew: יְיָ אֵל דֵּעוֹת
Transliteration: Ah-doe-nigh El Deh-oat
Translation: LORD God of Knowledge

This Chapter: Practice writing in Hebrew and saying aloud the Hebrew Title often. You can also make notes, list questions to research, etc.

LORD God of Knowledge .... יְיָ אֵל דֵּעוֹת

SIMPLY EV'REET | 31

Nehts-sakh Yees-rah-el .... נֵצַח יִשְׂרָאֵל

Chapter/Verse: I Samuel 15:29
Hebrew: נֵצַח יִשְׂרָאֵל
Transliteration: Nehts-sakh Yees-rah-el
Translation: Strength of Israel

Practice writing, saying Nehts-sakh Yees-rah-el.

NAME	SOUND		LETTER
Nun	n		נ
Tsade	ts		צ
Chet	Kh		ח
	nehts tsackh		נֵצַח
Yud	y		י
Sin	s		שׂ
	Yees		יִשְׂ
Resh	r		ר
	rah		רָ
Aleph	Silent		א
Lamed	l		ל
	el		אֵל

Nehts-sakh Yees-rah-el .... נֵצַח יִשְׂרָאֵל

Nehts-sakh Yees-rah-el .... נֵצַח יִשְׂרָאֵל

Chapter/Verse: I Samuel 15:29
Hebrew: נֵצַח יִשְׂרָאֵל
Transliteration: Nehts-sakh Yees-rah-el
Translation: Strength of Israel

This Chapter: Practice writing in Hebrew and saying aloud the Hebrew Title often. You can also make notes, list questions to research, etc.

Strength of Israel .... נֵצַח יִשְׂרָאֵל

_____

_____

_____

_____

_____

_____

_____

_____

_____

_____

_____

Ah-doe-nigh Nay-ree .... יְיָ נֵירִי

Chapter/Verse: II Samuel 22:29
Hebrew: יְיָ נֵירִי
Transliteration: Ah-doe-nigh Nay-ree
Translation: LORD my Light

Practice writing, saying Ah-doe-nigh Nay-ree.

NAME	SOUND		LETTER
Yud	y		יְ
	Ah-doe-nigh		יְיָ
Nun	n		נ
Yud	y		י
	Nay		נֵי
Resh	r		ר
Yud	y		י
	ree		רִי

Ah-doe-nigh Nay-ree .... יְיָ נֵירִי

Ah-doe-nigh Nay-ree .... יְיָ נֵירִי

Chapter/Verse: II Samuel 22:29
Hebrew: יְיָ נֵירִי
Transliteration: Ah-doe-nigh Nay-ree
Translation: LORD my Light

This Chapter: Practice writing in Hebrew and saying aloud the Hebrew Title often. You can also make notes, list questions to research, etc.

LORD my Light .... יְיָ נֵירִי

Ah-doe-nigh Eh-lo-hey Av-rah-ham Yeets-khak veh Yees-rah-el

יְיָ אֱלֹהֵי אַבְרָהָם יִצְחָק וְיִשְׂרָאֵל

Chapter/Verse:	I Kings 18:36
Hebrew:	יְיָ אֱלֹהֵי אַבְרָהָם יִצְחָק וְיִשְׂרָאֵל
Transliteration:	Ah-doe-nigh Eh-lo-hey Av-rah-ham Yeets-khak veh Yees-rah-el
Translation:	LORD God of Abraham, Isaac and Israel

Practice writing, saying Ah-doe-nigh Eh-lo-hey Av-rah-ham Yeets-khak veh Yees-rah-el.

NAME	SOUND		LETTER
Yud	y		י
	Ah-doe-nigh		יְיָ
Aleph	Silent		א
	Eh		אֱ
Lamed	l		ל
Cholem	lo		לֹ
Hey	h		ה
Yud	y		י
	hey		הֵי
Aleph	Silent		א
	ah		אַ
Vet	v		ב
	Ahv		אַבְ
Resh	r		ר
	rah		רָ

36 | SIMPLY EV'REET

Hey	h		ה
Final Mem	m		ם
	hahm		הָם
Yud	y		י
Tsade	ts		צ
	Yeets		יְצ
Chet	kh		ח
Kof	k		ק
	khak		חָק
Vav	v		ו
	veh		וְ
Yud	y		י
Sin	s		שׂ
	Yees		יִשׂ
Resh	r		ר
	rah		רָ
Aleph	Silent		א
Lamed	l		ל
	el		אֵל

Ah-doe-nigh Eh-lo-hey Av-rah-ham Yeets-khak veh Yees-rah-el

יְיָ אֱלֹהֵי אַבְרָהָם יִצְחָק וְיִשְׂרָאֵל ....

Ah-doe-nigh Eh-lo-hey Av-rah-ham Yeets-khak veh Yees-rah-el

יְיָ אֱלֹהֵי אַבְרָהָם יִצְחָק וְיִשְׂרָאֵל ....

Chapter/Verse:	I Kings 18:36
Hebrew:	יְיָ אֱלֹהֵי אַבְרָהָם יִצְחָק וְיִשְׂרָאֵל
Transliteration:	Ah-doe-nigh Eh-lo-hey Av-rah-ham Yeets-khak veh Yees-rah-el
Translation:	LORD God of Abraham, Isaac and Israel

This Chapter: Practice writing in Hebrew and saying aloud the Hebrew Title often. You can also make notes, list questions to research, etc.

LORD God of Abraham, Isaac and Israel ....

יְיָ אֱלֹהֵי אַבְרָהָם יִצְחָק וְיִשְׂרָאֵל
....

_____

_____

_____

_____

_____

_____

_____

_____

_____

Reflections

At this point in your study, consider taking time to reflect and think about why you have chosen to complete this *Simply Ev'reet Workbook Primer*. What goals did you set? Have they been met? Have your studies so far affected you in any way? What other comments do you have? Date and list your reflections before continuing your studies.

Date: _____

_____

_____

_____

_____

_____

_____

_____

_____

_____

_____

_____

_____

_____

_____

Eh-lo-hey ha-Ah-rehts .... אֱלֹהֵי הָאָרֶץ

Chapter/Verse: II Kings 17:26–27
Hebrew: אֱלֹהֵי הָאָרֶץ
Transliteration: Eh-lo-hey ha-Ah-rehts
Translation: God of the Earth

Practice writing, saying Eh-lo-hey ha-Ah-rehts.

NAME	SOUND		LETTER
Aleph	Silent		א
	Eh		אֶ
Lamed	l		ל
Cholem	lo		לֹ
Hey	h		ה
Yud	y		י
	hey		הֵי
Hey	h		ה
	ha		הָ
Aleph	Silent		א
	ah		אָ
Resh	r		ר
Final Tsade	ts		ץ
	rehts		רֶץ

Eh-lo-hey ha-Ah-rehts .... אֱלֹהֵי הָאָרֶץ

Eh-lo-hey ha-Ah-rehts .... אֱלֹהֵי הָאָרֶץ

Chapter/Verse: II Kings 17:26–27
Hebrew: אֱלֹהֵי הָאָרֶץ
Transliteration: Eh-lo-hey ha-Ah-rehts
Translation: God of the Earth

This Chapter: Practice writing in Hebrew and saying aloud the Hebrew Title often. You can also make notes, list questions to research, etc.

God of the Earth .... אֱלֹהֵי הָאָרֶץ

_____

_____

_____

_____

_____

_____

_____

_____

_____

_____

Peh-leh .... פֶּלֶא

Chapter/Verse: Isaiah 9:5
Hebrew: פֶּלֶא
Transliteration: Peh-leh
Translation: Wonderful

Practice writing, saying Peh-leh.

NAME	SOUND		LETTER
Pey	p		פ
	Peh		פֶּ
Lamed	l		ל
	leh		לֶ
Aleph	Silent		א

Peh-leh .... פֶּלֶא

Peh-leh .... פֶּלֶא

Chapter/Verse: Isaiah 9:5
Hebrew: פֶּלֶא
Transliteration: Peh-leh
Translation: Wonderful

This Chapter: Practice writing in Hebrew and saying aloud the Hebrew Title often. You can also make notes, list questions to research, etc.

Wonderful .... פֶּלֶא

_____

_____

_____

_____

_____

_____

_____

_____

_____

_____

Yo-ehts .... יוֹעֵץ

Chapter/Verse: Isaiah 9:5
Hebrew: יוֹעֵץ
Transliteration: Yo-ehts
Translation: Counselor

Practice writing, saying Yo-ehts.

NAME	SOUND		LETTER
Yud	y		י
	oh		וֹ
	Yo		יוֹ
Ayin	Silent		ע
	eh		עֵ
Final Tsade	ts		ץ
	ehts		עֵץ

Yo-ehts .... יוֹעֵץ

Yo-ehts .... יוֹעֵץ

Chapter/Verse: Isaiah 9:5
Hebrew: יוֹעֵץ
Transliteration: Yo-ehts
Translation: Counselor

This Chapter: Practice writing in Hebrew and saying aloud the Hebrew Title often. You can also make notes, list questions to research, etc.

Counselor .... יוֹעֵץ

_____
_____
_____
_____
_____
_____
_____
_____
_____
_____
_____

El-Ghee-bor .... אֵל גִּבּוֹר

Chapter/Verse: Isaiah 9:5
Hebrew: אֵל גִּבּוֹר
Transliteration: El-Ghee-bor
Translation: Mighty God

Practice writing, saying El-Ghee-bor.

NAME	SOUND		LETTER
Aleph	Silent		א
Lamed	l		ל
	Ehl		אֵל
Gimel	g		ג
	Ghee		גִּ
Bet	b		בּ
Cholem Vav	oh		וֹ
Resh	r		ר
	bor		בּוֹר

El-Ghee-bor .... אֵל גִּבּוֹר

El-Ghee-bor.. אֵל גִּבּוֹר

Chapter/Verse: Isaiah 9:5
Hebrew: אֵל גִּבּוֹר
Transliteration: El-Ghee-bor
Translation: Mighty God

This Chapter: Practice writing in Hebrew and saying aloud the Hebrew Title often. You can also make notes, list questions to research, etc.

Mighty God.. אֵל גִּבּוֹר

_____

_____

_____

_____

_____

_____

_____

_____

_____

_____

_____

_____

_____

Ah-vee Ahd .... אֲבִי־עַד

Chapter/Verse: Isaiah 9:5
Hebrew: אֲבִי־עַד
Transliteration: Ah-vee Ahd
Translation: Eternal Father

Practice writing, saying Ah-vee Ahd.

NAME	SOUND		LETTER
Aleph	Silent		א
	Ah		אַ
Vet	v		ב
Yud	y		י
	vee		בִי
Ayin	Silent		ע
	ah		עַ
Dalet	d		ד
	Ahd		עַד

Ah-vee Ahd .... אֲבִי־עַד

Ah-vee Ahd .... אֲבִי־עַד

Chapter/Verse: Isaiah 9:5
Hebrew: אֲבִי־עַד
Transliteration: Ah-vee Ahd
Translation: Eternal Father

This Chapter: Practice writing in Hebrew and saying aloud the Hebrew Title often. You can also make notes, list questions to research, etc.

Eternal Father .... אֲבִי־עַד

_____

_____

_____

_____

_____

_____

_____

_____

_____

_____

_____

Sar Sha-lom .... שַׂר שָׁלוֹם

Chapter/Verse: Isaiah 9:5
Hebrew: שַׂר שָׁלוֹם
Transliteration: Sar Sha-lom
Translation: Prince of Peace

Practice writing, saying Sar Sha-lom.

NAME	SOUND		LETTER
Sin	s		שׂ
Resh	r		ר
	Sar		שַׂר
Shin	sh		שׁ
	Sha		שָׁ
Lamed	l		ל
Cholem Vav	oh		וֹ
Final Mem	m		ם
	lom		לוֹם

Sar Sha-lom .... שַׂר שָׁלוֹם

Sar Sha-lom .... שַׂר שָׁלוֹם

Chapter/Verse: Isaiah 9:5
Hebrew: שַׂר שָׁלוֹם
Transliteration: Sar Sha-lom
Translation: Prince of Peace

This Chapter: Practice writing in Hebrew and saying aloud the Hebrew Title often. You can also make notes, list questions to research, etc.

Prince of Peace .... שַׂר שָׁלוֹם

Meh-lekh ha Go-yeem .... מֶלֶךְ הַגּוֹיִם

Chapter/Verse: Jeremiah 10:7
Hebrew: מֶלֶךְ הַגּוֹיִם
Transliteration: Meh-lekh ha Go-yeem
Translation: King of the Nations

Practice writing, saying Meh-lekh ha Go-yeem.

NAME	SOUND		LETTER
Mem	m		מ
	Meh		מֶ
Lamed	l		ל
Final Kaf	k		ךְ
	kh		ךְ
Hey	h		ה
	ha		הַ
Gimmel	g		ג
Cholem Vav	oh		וֹ
	Go		גוֹ
Yud	y		י
Final Mem	m		ם
	yeem		יִם

Meh-lekh ha Go-yeem .... מֶלֶךְ הַגּוֹיִם

Meh-lekh ha Go-yeem .... מֶלֶךְ הַגּוֹיִם

Chapter/Verse: Jeremiah 10:7
Hebrew: מֶלֶךְ הַגּוֹיִם
Transliteration: Meh-lekh ha Go-yeem
Translation: King of the Nations

This Chapter: Practice writing in Hebrew and saying aloud the Hebrew Title often. You can also make notes, list questions to research, etc.

King of the Nations .... מֶלֶךְ הַגּוֹיִם

_____

_____

_____

_____

_____

_____

_____

_____

_____

_____

Ah-doe-nigh Tseed-kay-new .... יְיָ צִדְקֵנוּ

Chapter/Verse: Jeremiah 23:6
Hebrew: יְיָ צִדְקֵנוּ
Transliteration: Ah-doe-nigh Tseed-kay-new
Translation: LORD our Righteousness

Practice writing, saying Ah-doe-nigh Tseed-kay-new.

NAME	SOUND		LETTER
	Ah-doe-nigh		יְיָ
Tsade	ts		צ
Dalet	d		ד
	Tseed		צִד
Kaf	k		ק
	kay		קֵ
Nun	n		נ
	new		נוּ

Ah-doe-nigh Tseed-kay-new .... יְיָ צִדְקֵנוּ

Ah-doe-nigh Tseed-kay-new .... יְיָ צִדְקֵנוּ

Chapter/Verse: Jeremiah 23:6
Hebrew: יְיָ צִדְקֵנוּ
Transliteration: Ah-doe-nigh Tseed-kay-new
Translation: LORD our Righteousness

This Chapter: Practice writing in Hebrew and saying aloud the Hebrew Title often. You can also make notes, list questions to research, etc.

LORD our Righteousness .... יְיָ צִדְקֵנוּ

Ah-doe-nigh Ah-doe-nigh............................אֲדֹנָי יְיָ

Chapter/Verse: Ezekiel 47:23
Hebrew: אֲדֹנָי יְיָ
Transliteration: Ah-doe-nigh Ah-doe-nigh
Translation: Lord GOD

Practice writing, saying Ah-doe-nigh Ah-doe-nigh.

NAME	SOUND		LETTER
Aleph	Silent		א
	Ah		אַ
Dalet	d		ד
Cholem	doe		דֹ
Nun	n		נ
	nigh		נָי
	Ah-doe-nigh		יְיָ

Ah-doe-nigh Ah-doe-nigh......................אֲדֹנָי יְיָ

56 | SIMPLY EV'REET

Ah-doe-nigh Ah-doe-nigh .... אֲדֹנָי יְיָ

Chapter/Verse: Ezekiel 47:23
Hebrew: אֲדֹנָי יְיָ
Transliteration: Ah-doe-nigh Ah-doe-nigh
Translation: Lord GOD

This Chapter: Practice writing in Hebrew and saying aloud the Hebrew Title often. You can also make notes, list questions to research, etc.

Lord GOD .... אֲדֹנָי יְיָ

_____

_____

_____

_____

_____

_____

_____

_____

_____

_____

Ah-doe-nigh Shah-mah .... יְיָ שָׁמָּה

Chapter/Verse: Ezekiel 48:35
Hebrew: יְיָ שָׁמָּה
Transliteration: Ah-doe-nigh Shah-mah
Translation: LORD is There

Practice writing, saying Ah-doe-nigh Shah-mah.

NAME	SOUND		LETTER
	Ah-doe-nigh		יְיָ
Shin	sh		שׁ
	Shah		שָׁ
Mem	m		מ
Hey	h		ה
	mah		מָה

Ah-doe-nigh Shah-mah .... יְיָ שָׁמָּה

Ah-doe-nigh Shah-mah............ יְיָ שָׁמָּה

Chapter/Verse: Ezekiel 48:35
Hebrew: יְיָ שָׁמָּה
Transliteration: Ah-doe-nigh Shah-mah
Translation: LORD is There

This Chapter: Practice writing in Hebrew and saying aloud the Hebrew Title often. You can also make notes, list questions to research, etc.

LORD is There............ יְיָ שָׁמָּה

_____

_____

_____

_____

_____

_____

_____

_____

_____

_____

Ah-doe-nigh Ee-she .... יְיָ אִישִׁי

Chapter/Verse: Hosea 2:18
Hebrew: יְיָ אִישִׁי
Transliteration: Ah-doe-nigh Ee-she
Translation: LORD my Husband

Practice writing, saying Ah-doe-nigh Ee-she.

NAME	SOUND		LETTER
	Ah-doe-nigh		יְיָ
Aleph	Silent		א
Yud	y		י
	Ee		אִי
Shin	sh		שׁ
Yud	y		י
	she		שִׁי

Ah-doe-nigh Ee-she .... יְיָ אִישִׁי

Ah-doe-nigh Ee-she .... יִ֣י אִישִׁ֔י

Chapter/Verse: Hosea 2:18
Hebrew: יִ֣י אִישִׁ֔י
Transliteration: Ah-doe-nigh Ee-she
Translation: LORD my Husband

This Chapter: Practice writing in Hebrew and saying aloud the Hebrew Title often. You can also make notes, list questions to research, etc.

LORD my Husband .... יִ֣י אִישִׁ֔י

_____

_____

_____

_____

_____

_____

_____

_____

_____

_____

_____

(vah)Ah-doe-nigh Mah-kha-seh ooh-Mah-ohz
יְיָ מַחֲסֶה וּמָעוֹז............

Chapter/Verse:	Joel 3:16
Hebrew:	יְיָ מַחֲסֶה וּמָעוֹז
Transliteration:	(vah)Ah-doe-nigh Mah-kha-seh ooh-Mah-ohz
Translation:	(and) LORD (is a) Refuge (and) Strength

Practice writing, saying (vah)Ah-doe-nigh Mah-kha-seh ooh-Mah-ohz.

NAME	SOUND		LETTER
	Ah-doe-nigh		יְיָ
Mem	m		מ
	Mah		מַ
Chet	kh		ח
	kha		חֲ
Samekh	s		ס
Hey	h		ה
	seh		סֶה
Vav	v		ו
Shureq	ooh		וּ
	Mah		מָ
Ayin	Silent		ע
Vav	v		ו
Cholem Vav	oh		וֹ
Zayin	z		ז
	ohz		וֹז

(vah)Ah-doe-nigh Mah-kha-seh ooh-Mah-ohz....... יְיָ מַחֲסֶה וּמָעוֹז

(vah)Ah-doe-nigh Mah-kha-seh ooh-Mah-ohz
יְיָ מַחְסֶה וּמָעוֹז ....

Chapter/Verse:	Joel 3:16
Hebrew:	יְיָ מַחְסֶה וּמָעוֹז
Transliteration:	(vah)Ah-doe-nigh Mah-kha-seh ooh-Mah-ohz
Translation:	(and) LORD (is a) Refuge (and) Strength

This Chapter: Practice writing in Hebrew and saying aloud the Hebrew Title often. You can also make notes, list questions to research, etc.

(and) LORD (is a) Refuge (and) Strength .... יְיָ מַחְסֶה וּמָעוֹז

_____

_____

_____

_____

_____

_____

_____

_____

_____

_____

SIMPLY EV'REET

Ah-doe-nigh Ah-doe-nigh Eh-lo-hey hahTs-vah-oat
אֲדֹנָי יְיָ אֱלֹהֵי הַצְּבָאוֹת

Chapter/Verse: Amos 3:13
Hebrew: אֲדֹנָי יְיָ אֱלֹהֵי הַצְּבָאוֹת
Transliteration: Ah-doe-nigh Ah-doe-nigh Eh-lo-hey hahTs-vah-oat
Translation: Lord GOD God of Hosts

Practice writing, saying Ah-doe-nigh Ah-doe-nigh Eh-lo-hey hahTs-vah-oat.

NAME	SOUND		LETTER
Aleph	Silent		א
	ah		אַ
Dalet	d		ד
Cholem	doe		דֹ
Nun	n		נ
Yud	y		י
	nigh		נָי
	Ah-doe-nigh		אֲדֹנָי
Aleph	Silent		א
	eh		אֱ

Lamed	l		ל
Cholem	lo		לֹ
Hey	h		ה
Yud	y		י
	hey		הֵי
Hey	h		ה
	hah		הַ
Tsade	ts		צ
	hahTs		הַצְ
Vet	v		ב
	vah		בָ
Cholem Vav	oh		וֹ
Tav	t		ת
	oat		וֹת

Ah-doe-nigh Ah-doe-nigh Eh-lo-hey hahTs-vah-oat

אֲדֹנָי יְיָ אֱלֹהֵי הַצְּבָאוֹת ....

Ah-doe-nigh Ah-doe-nigh Eh-lo-hey hahTs-vah-oat
אֲדֹנָי יְיָ אֱלֹהֵי הַצְּבָאוֹת ....

Chapter/Verse:	Amos 3:13
Hebrew:	אֲדֹנָי יְיָ אֱלֹהֵי הַצְּבָאוֹת
Transliteration:	Ah-doe-nigh Ah-doe-nigh Eh-lo-hey hahTs-vah-oat
Translation:	Lord GOD God of Hosts

This Chapter: Practice writing in Hebrew and saying aloud the Hebrew Title often. You can also make notes, list questions to research, etc.

Lord GOD God of Hosts .... אֲדֹנָי יְיָ אֱלֹהֵי הַצְּבָאוֹת

___

___

___

___

___

___

___

___

___

___

Reflections

At this point in your study, consider taking time to reflect and think about why you have chosen to complete this *Simply Ev'reet Workbook Primer.* What goals did you set? Have they been met? Have your studies so far affected you in any way? From memory, what Names are you able to write in Hebrew? What other comments do you have? Date and list your reflections before continuing your studies.

Date: _____

_____

_____

_____

_____

_____

_____

_____

_____

_____

_____

_____

_____

Ah-doe-nigh .... אֲדֹנָי

Chapter/Verse: Obadiah 1:15*
Hebrew: אֲדֹנָי
Transliteration: Ah-doe-nigh
Translation: LORD/GOD

Practice writing, saying Ah-doe-nigh.

NAME	SOUND		LETTER
	Ah-doe-nigh		אֲדֹנָי

Ah-doe-nigh .... אֲדֹנָי

*see also Obadiah 1:1

Ah-doe-nigh .... יְיָ

Chapter/Verse: Obadiah 1:15
Hebrew: יְיָ
Transliteration: Ah-doe-nigh
Translation: LORD/GOD

This Chapter: Practice writing in Hebrew and saying aloud the Hebrew Title often. You can also make notes, list questions to research, etc.

LORD/GOD .... יְיָ

_____

_____

_____

_____

_____

_____

_____

_____

_____

_____

_____

Ah-doe-nigh Eh-lo-hey ha-Shah-mah-yeem
יְיָ אֱלֹהֵי הַשָּׁמַיִם

Chapter/Verse: Jonah 1:9
Hebrew: יְיָ אֱלֹהֵי הַשָּׁמַיִם
Transliteration: Ah-doe-nigh Eh-lo-hey ha-Shah-mah-yeem
Translation: LORD God of Heaven

Practice writing, saying Ah-doe-nigh Eh-lo-hey-ha-Shah-mah-yeem.

NAME	SOUND		LETTER
	Ah-doe-nigh		יְיָ
Aleph	Silent		א
	Eh		אֶ
Lamed	l		ל
Cholem	lo		לֹ
Hey	h		ה
	hey		הֵי
Hey	h		ה
	ha		הַ
Shin	sh		שׁ
	Shah		שָׁ
Mem	m		מ
	mah		מַ
Yud	y		י
Final Mem	m		ם
	yeem		יִם

Ah-doe-nigh Eh-lo-hey ha-Shah-mah-yeem .... יְיָ אֱלֹהֵי הַשָּׁמַיִם

Ah-doe-nigh Eh-lo-hey ha-Shah-mah-yeem
יְיָ אֱלֹהֵי הַשָּׁמַיִם

Chapter/Verse:	Jonah 1:9
Hebrew:	יְיָ אֱלֹהֵי הַשָּׁמַיִם
Transliteration:	Ah-doe-nigh Eh-lo hey-ha-Shah-mah-yeem
Translation:	LORD God of Heaven

This Chapter: Practice writing in Hebrew and saying aloud the Hebrew Title often. You can also make notes, list questions to research, etc.

LORD God of Heaven .... יְיָ אֱלֹהֵי הַשָּׁמַיִם

_____

_____

_____

_____

_____

_____

_____

_____

_____

Eh-lo-hey Yah-ah-kov .... אֱלֹהֵי יַעֲקֹב

Chapter/Verse: Micah 4:2
Hebrew: אֱלֹהֵי יַעֲקֹב
Transliteration: Eh-lo-hey Yah-ah-kov
Translation: God of Jacob

Practice writing, saying Eh-lo-hey Yah-ah-kov.

NAME	SOUND		LETTER
Aleph	Silent		א
	Eh		אֶ
Lamed	l		לֹ
Cholem	lo		לֹ
Hey	h		ה
Yud	y		י
	hey		הֵי
Yud	y		י
	Yah		יַ
Ayin	Silent		ע
	ah		עֲ
Kof	k		ק
Vet	v		ב
Cholem	kov		קֹב

Eh-lo-hey Yah-ah-kov .... אֱלֹהֵי יַעֲקֹב

Eh-lo-hey Yah-ah-kov .... אֱלֹהֵי יַעֲקֹב

Chapter/Verse: Micah 4:2
Hebrew: אֱלֹהֵי יַעֲקֹב
Transliteration: Eh-lo-hey Yah-ah-kov
Translation: God of Jacob

This Chapter: Practice writing in Hebrew and saying aloud the Hebrew Title often. You can also make notes, list questions to research, etc.

God of Jacob .... אֱלֹהֵי יַעֲקֹב

_____

_____

_____

_____

_____

_____

_____

_____

_____

_____

Ah-doe-nigh Or-lee .... יְיָ אוֹר לִי

Chapter/Verse: Micah 7:8
Hebrew: יְיָ אוֹר לִי
Transliteration: Ah-doe-nigh Or-lee
Translation: LORD Light to me/LORD (is my) Light

Practice writing, saying Ah-doe-nigh Or-lee.

NAME	SOUND		LETTER
	Ah-doe-nigh		יְיָ
Aleph	Silent		א
Cholem Vav	oh		וֹ
Resh	r		ר
	Or		אוֹר
Lamed	l		ל
Yud	y		י
	lee		לִי

Ah-doe-nigh Or-lee .... יְיָ אוֹר לִי

Ah-doe-nigh Or-lee .... יְיָ אוֹר לִי

Chapter/Verse: Micah 7:8
Hebrew: יְיָ אוֹר לִי
Transliteration: Ah-doe-nigh Or-lee
Translation: LORD Light to me/LORD (is my) Light

This Chapter: Practice writing in Hebrew and saying aloud the Hebrew Title often. You can also make notes, list questions to research, etc.

LORD Light to me/LORD (is my) Light .... יְיָ אוֹר לִי

Ah-doe-nigh Tseh-vah-oat .... יְיָ צְבָאוֹת

Chapter/Verse: Nahum 3:5
Hebrew: יְיָ צְבָאוֹת
Transliteration: Ah-doe-nigh Tseh-vah-oat
Translation: LORD of Hosts (Armies)

Practice writing, saying Ah-doe-nigh Tseh-vah-oat.

NAME	SOUND		LETTER
	Ah-doe-nigh		יְיָ
Tsade	ts		צ
	Tseh		צְ
Vet	v		ב
	vah		בָ
Cholem Vav	oh		וֹ
Tav	t		ת
	oat		וֹת

Ah-doe-nigh Tseh-vah-oat .... יְיָ צְבָאוֹת

Ah-doe-nigh Tseh-vah-oat .... יְיָ צְבָאוֹת

Chapter/Verse: Nahum 3:5
Hebrew: יְיָ צְבָאוֹת
Transliteration: Ah-doe-nigh Tseh-vah-oat
Translation: LORD of Hosts (Armies)

This Chapter: Practice writing in Hebrew and saying aloud the Hebrew Title often. You can also make notes, list questions to research, etc.

LORD of Hosts (Armies) .... יְיָ צְבָאוֹת

_____

_____

_____

_____

_____

_____

_____

_____

_____

_____

Ah-doe-nigh Eh-lo-high Keh-doe-shee....... יְיָ אֱלֹהַי קְדֹשִׁי

Chapter/Verse: Habakkuk 1:12
Hebrew: יְיָ אֱלֹהַי קְדֹשִׁי
Transliteration: Ah-doe-nigh Eh-lo-high Keh-doe-shee
Translation: LORD my God, my Holy One

Practice writing, saying Ah-doe-nigh Eh-lo-high Keh-doe-shee.

NAME	SOUND		LETTER
	Ah-doe-nigh		יְיָ
Aleph	Silent		א
	Eh		אֶ
Lamed	l		ל
Cholem	lo		לֹ
Hey	h		ה
Yud	y		י
	hi		הַי
Kof	k		ק
	Keh		קְ
Dalet	d		ד
Cholem	doe		דֹ
Shin	sh		שׁ
	shee		שִׁי

Ah-doe-nigh Eh-lo-high Keh-doe-shee........ יְיָ אֱלֹהַי קְדֹשִׁי

Ah-doe-nigh Eh-lo-high Keh-doe-shee....... יְיָ אֱלֹהַי קְדֹשִׁי

Chapter/Verse:	Habakkuk 1:12
Hebrew:	יְיָ אֱלֹהַי קְדֹשִׁי
Transliteration:	Ah-doe-nigh Eh-lo-high Keh-doe-shee
Translation:	LORD my God, my Holy One

This Chapter: Practice writing in Hebrew and saying aloud the Hebrew Title often. You can also make notes, list questions to research, etc.

LORD my God, my Holy One .... יְיָ אֱלֹהַי קְדֹשִׁי

SIMPLY EV'REET

Ah-doe-nigh Eh-lo-high-yeech .... יְיָ אֱלֹהַיִךְ

Chapter/Verse: Zephaniah 3:17
Hebrew: יְיָ אֱלֹהַיִךְ
Transliteration: Ah-doe-nigh Eh-lo-high-yeech
Translation: LORD your God (FS)

Practice writing, saying Ah-doe-nigh Eh-lo-high-yeech.

NAME	SOUND		LETTER
	Ah-doe-nigh		יְיָ
Aleph	Silent		א
	Eh		אֱ
Lamed	l		ל
Cholem	lo		לֹ
Hey	h		ה
	high		הַ
Yud	y		י
Final Kaf	k		ךְ
	yeech		יִךְ

Ah-doe-nigh Eh-lo-high-yeech .... יְיָ אֱלֹהַיִךְ

Ah-doe-nigh Eh-lo-high-yeech .... יְיָ אֱלֹהַיִךְ

Chapter/Verse: Zephaniah 3:17
Hebrew: יְיָ אֱלֹהַיִךְ
Transliteration: Ah-doe-nigh Eh-lo-high-yeech
Translation: LORD your God (FS)

This Chapter: Practice writing in Hebrew and saying aloud the Hebrew Title often. You can also make notes, list questions to research, etc.

LORD your God .... יְיָ אֱלֹהַיִךְ

_____

_____

_____

_____

_____

_____

_____

_____

_____

_____

_____

Eh-lo-hey-hehm .... אֱלֹהֵיהֶם

Chapter/Verse: Haggai 1:14
Hebrew: אֱלֹהֵיהֶם
Transliteration: Eh-lo-hey-hehm
Translation: Their God

Practice writing, saying Eh-lo-hey-hehm.

NAME	SOUND		LETTER
Aleph	Silent		א
	Eh		אֱ
Lamed	l		ל
Cholem	lo		לֹ
Hey	h		ה
Yud	y		י
	hey		הֵי
Hey	h		ה
Final Mem	m		ם
	hehm		הֶם

Eh-lo-hey-hehm .... אֱלֹהֵיהֶם

Eh-lo-hey-hehm .... אֱלֹהֵיהֶם

Chapter/Verse: Haggai 1:14
Hebrew: אֱלֹהֵיהֶם
Transliteration: Eh-lo-hey-hehm
Translation: Their God

This Chapter: Practice writing in Hebrew and saying aloud the Hebrew Title often. You can also make notes, list questions to research, etc.

Their God .... אֱלֹהֵיהֶם

_____

_____

_____

_____

_____

_____

_____

_____

_____

_____

_____

Tseh-mahk .... צֶמַח

Chapter/Verse: Zechariah 3:8
Hebrew: צֶמַח
Transliteration: Tseh-mahk
Translation: Branch

Practice writing, saying Tseh-mahk.

NAME	SOUND		LETTER
Tsade	ts		צ
	Tseh		צֶ
Mem	m		מ
Chet	kh		ח
	mahk		מַח

Tseh-mahk .... צֶמַח

Tseh-mahk .... צֶמַח

Chapter/Verse: Zechariah 3:8
Hebrew: צֶמַח
Transliteration: Tseh-mahk
Translation: Branch

This Chapter: Practice writing in Hebrew and saying aloud the Hebrew Title often. You can also make notes, list questions to research, etc.

Branch .... צֶמַח

_____

_____

_____

_____

_____

_____

_____

_____

_____

_____

_____

Eh-lo-hey ha-Meesh-paht .... אֱלֹהֵי הַמִּשְׁפָּט

Chapter/Verse: Malachi 2:17
Hebrew: אֱלֹהֵי הַמִּשְׁפָּט
Transliteration: Eh-lo-hey ha-Meesh-paht
Translation: God of Judgment

Practice writing, saying Eh-lo-hey ha-Meesh-paht.

NAME	SOUND		LETTER
Aleph	Silent		א
	Eh		אֶ
Lamed	l		ל
Cholem	lo		לֹ
Hey	h		ה
Yud	y		י
	hey		הֵי
Hey	h		ה
	ha		הַ
Mem	m		מ
Shin	sh		שׁ
	Meesh		מִּשׁ
Pey	p		פּ
Tet	t		ט
	paht		פָּט

Eh-lo-hey ha-Meesh-paht .... אֱלֹהֵי הַמִּשְׁפָּט

Eh-lo-hey ha-Meesh-paht .... אֱלֹהֵי הַמִּשְׁפָּט

Chapter/Verse: Malachi 2:17
Hebrew: אֱלֹהֵי הַמִּשְׁפָּט
Transliteration: Eh-lo-hey ha-Meesh-paht
Translation: God of Judgment

This Chapter: Practice writing in Hebrew and saying aloud the Hebrew Title often. You can also make notes, list questions to research, etc.

God of Judgment .... אֱלֹהֵי הַמִּשְׁפָּט

_____

_____

_____

_____

_____

_____

_____

_____

_____

_____

El-yon..עֶלְיוֹן

Chapter/Verse: Psalms 9:3
Hebrew: עֶלְיוֹן
Transliteration: El-yon
Translation: Most High

Practice writing, saying El-yon.

NAME	SOUND		LETTER
Ayin	Silent		ע
	eh		עֶ
Lamed	l		ל
	El		עֶל
Yud	y		י
Cholem Vav	oh		וֹ
Final Nun	n		ן
	yon		יוֹן

El-yon..עֶלְיוֹן

88 | SIMPLY EV'REET

El-yon .... עֶלְיוֹן

Chapter/Verse: Psalms 9:3
Hebrew: עֶלְיוֹן
Transliteration: El-yon
Translation: Most High

This Chapter: Practice writing in Hebrew and saying aloud the Hebrew Title often. You can also make notes, list questions to research, etc.

Most High .... עֶלְיוֹן

_____

_____

_____

_____

_____

_____

_____

_____

_____

_____

Eh-lo-heh-hah .... אֱלֹהֶיהָ

Chapter/Verse: Proverbs 2:17
Hebrew: אֱלֹהֶיהָ
Transliteration: Eh-lo-heh-hah
Translation: Her God

Practice writing, saying Eh-lo-heh-hah.

NAME	SOUND		LETTER
Aleph	Silent		א
	Eh		אֶ
Lamed	l		ל
Cholem	lo		לֹ
Hey	h		ה
Yud	y		י
	heh		הֶי
Hey	h		ה
	hah		הָ

Eh-lo-heh-hah .... אֱלֹהֶיהָ

Eh-lo-heh-hah .... אֱלֹהֶיהָ

Chapter/Verse: Proverbs 2:17
Hebrew: אֱלֹהֶיהָ
Transliteration: Eh-lo-heh-hah
Translation: Her God

This Chapter: Practice writing in Hebrew and saying aloud the Hebrew Title often. You can also make notes, list questions to research, etc.

Her God .... אֱלֹהֶיהָ

Shah-dye .... שַׁדַּי

Chapter/Verse: Job 5:17
Hebrew: שַׁדַּי
Transliteration: Shah-dye
Translation: Almighty

Practice writing, saying Shah-dye.

NAME	SOUND		LETTER
Shin	sh		שׁ
	Shah		שַׁ
Dalet	d		ד
Yud	y		י
	dye		דַּי

Shah-dye .... שַׁדַּי

Shah-dye .... שַׁדַּי

Chapter/Verse: Job 5:17
Hebrew: שַׁדַּי
Transliteration: Shah-dye
Translation: Almighty

This Chapter: Practice writing in Hebrew and saying aloud the Hebrew Title often. You can also make notes, list questions to research, etc.

Almighty .... שַׁדַּי

_____

_____

_____

_____

_____

_____

_____

_____

_____

_____

Go-ah-lee... גֹּאֲלִי

Chapter/Verse: Job 19:25
Hebrew: גֹּאֲלִי
Transliteration: Go-ah-lee
Translation: My Redeemer

Practice writing, saying Go-ah-lee.

NAME	SOUND		LETTER
Gimel	g		גּ
	Go		גֹּ
Aleph	Silent		א
	ah		אֲ
Lamed	l		ל
Yud	y		י
	lee		לִי

Go-ah-lee... גֹּאֲלִי

Go-ah-lee.. גֹּאֲלִי

Chapter/Verse: Job 19:25
Hebrew: גֹּאֲלִי
Transliteration: Go-ah-lee
Translation: My Redeemer

This Chapter: Practice writing in Hebrew and saying aloud the Hebrew Title often. You can also make notes, list questions to research, etc.

My Redeemer.. גֹּאֲלִי

(Ah-doe-nigh) Doe-dee .... (אֲדֹנָי) דּוֹדִי

Chapter/Verse:	Song of Songs 8:14
Hebrew:	(אֲדֹנָי) דּוֹדִי
Transliteration:	(Ah-doe-nigh) Doe-dee
Translation:	(Lord) My Beloved

Practice writing, saying (Ah-doe-nigh) Doe-dee.

NAME	SOUND		LETTER
Aleph	Silent		א
	ah		אֲ
Dalet	d		ד
	doe		דּ
Nun	n		נ
Yud	y		י
	nigh		נָי
Dalet	d		ד
	Doe		דּוֹ
Dalet	d		ד
	dee		דִי

(Ah-doe-nigh) Doe-dee .... (אֲדֹנָי) דּוֹדִי

(Ah-doe-nigh) Doe-dee .... (אֲדֹנָי) דּוֹדִי

Chapter/Verse: Song of Songs 8:14
Hebrew: (אֲדֹנָי) דּוֹדִי
Transliteration: (Ah-doe-nigh) Doe-dee
Translation: (Lord) My Beloved

This Chapter: Practice writing in Hebrew and saying aloud the Hebrew Title often. You can also make notes, list questions to research, etc.

(Lord) My Beloved .... (אֲדֹנָי)* דּוֹדִי

_____

_____

_____

_____

_____

_____

_____

_____

_____

_____

* Author's variation

(veh)Eh-lo-high-yeek Eh-lo-high....... וֵאלֹהַיִךְ אֱלֹהָי

Chapter/Verse:	Ruth 1:16
Hebrew:	וֵאלֹהַיִךְ אֱלֹהָי
Transliteration:	(veh)Eh-lo-high-yeek Eh-lo-high
Translation:	(and) Your God, My God (FS)

Practice writing, saying (veh)Eh-lo-high-yeek Eh-lo-high.

NAME	SOUND		LETTER
Aleph	Silent		א
	Eh		אֶ
Lamed	l		ל
Cholem	lo		לֹ
Hey	h		ה
	high		הַי
Yud	y		יִ
Final Kaf	k		ךְ
	yeek		יִךְ
Aleph	Silent		א
	Eh		אֱ
Lamed	l		ל
Cholem	lo		לֹ
Hey	h		ה
	high		הָי

(veh)Eh-lo-high-yeek Eh-lo-high......... וֵאלֹהַיִךְ אֱלֹהָי

(veh)Eh-lo-high-yeek Eh-lo-high .... וֵאלֹהַיִךְ אֱלֹהָי

Chapter/Verse: Ruth 1:16
Hebrew: וֵאלֹהַיִךְ אֱלֹהָי
Transliteration: (veh)Eh-lo-high-yeek Eh-lo-high
Translation: (and) Your God, My God (FS)

This Chapter: Practice writing in Hebrew and saying aloud the Hebrew Title often. You can also make notes, list questions to research, etc.

Your God, My God (FS) .... וֵאלֹהַיִךְ אֱלֹהָי

_____

_____

_____

_____

_____

_____

_____

_____

_____

_____

Ah-doe-nigh Eh-lo-hey Yees-rah-el .... יְיָ אֱלֹהֵי יִשְׂרָאֵל

Chapter/Verse: Ruth 2:12
Hebrew: יְיָ אֱלֹהֵי יִשְׂרָאֵל
Transliteration: Ah-doe-nigh Eh-lo-hey Yees-rah-el
Translation: LORD God of Israel

Practice writing, saying Ah-doe-nigh Eh-lo-hey Yees-rah-el.

NAME	SOUND		LETTER
	Ah-doe-nigh		יְיָ
Aleph	Silent		א
	Eh		אֶ
Lamed	l		ל
Cholem	lo		לֹ
Hey	h		ה
Yud	y		י
	hey		הֵי
Yud	y		י
Sin	s		שׂ
	Yees		יִשׂ
Resh	r		ר
	rah		רָ
Aleph	Silent		א
Lamed	l		ל
	el		אֵל

Ah-doe-nigh Eh-lo-hey Yees-rah-el .... יְיָ אֱלֹהֵי יִשְׂרָאֵל

Ah-doe-nigh Eh-lo-hey Yees-rah-el .... יְיָ אֱלֹהֵי יִשְׂרָאֵל

Chapter/Verse: Ruth 2:12
Hebrew: יְיָ אֱלֹהֵי יִשְׂרָאֵל
Transliteration: Ah-doe-nigh Eh-lo-hey Yees-rah-el
Translation: LORD God of Israel

This Chapter: Practice writing in Hebrew and saying aloud the Hebrew Title often. You can also make notes, list questions to research, etc.

LORD God of Israel .... יְיָ אֱלֹהֵי יִשְׂרָאֵל

El El .... אֶל־אֵל

Chapter/Verse: Lamentations 3:41
Hebrew: אֶל־אֵל
Transliteration: El El
Translation: To/For God

Practice writing, saying El El.

NAME	SOUND		LETTER
Aleph	Silent		א
Lamed	l		ל
	El		אֵל
Aleph	Silent		א
	eh		אֶ
Lamed	l		ל
	El		אֶל

El El .... אֶל־אֵל

SIMPLY EV'REET

El El .... אֶל־אֵל

Chapter/Verse: Lamentations 3:41
Hebrew: אֶל־אֵל
Transliteration: El El
Translation: To/For God

This Chapter: Practice writing in Hebrew and saying aloud the Hebrew Title often. You can also make notes, list questions to research, etc.

To/For God .... אֶל־אֵל

Bor-eh-kha .... בּוֹרְאֶיךָ

Chapter/Verse: Ecclesiastes 12:1
Hebrew: בּוֹרְאֶיךָ
Transliteration: Bor-eh-kha
Translation: Your Creator

Practice writing, saying Bor-eh-kha.

NAME	SOUND		LETTER
Bet	b		בּ
Cholem Vav	oh		וֹ
Resh	r		ר
	Bor		בּוֹר
Aleph	Silent		א
	eh		אֶי
Final Kaf	k		ךָ
	kha		ךָ

Bor-eh-kha .... בּוֹרְאֶיךָ

Bor-eh-kha .... בּוֹרְאֶיךָ

Chapter/Verse: Ecclesiastes 12:1
Hebrew: בּוֹרְאֶיךָ
Transliteration: Bor-eh-kha
Translation: Your Creator

This Chapter: Practice writing in Hebrew and saying aloud the Hebrew Title often. You can also make notes, list questions to research, etc.

Your Creator .... בּוֹרְאֶיךָ

Book .... Esther

Note: Although the God of Israel is implied, no Name is written in the book of Esther.

Book .... Esther

Note: Although the God of Israel is implied, no Name is written in the book of Esther.

Ah-doe-nigh ha-El ha-Gah-dol veh-ha No-rah
אֲדֹנָי הָאֵל הַגָּדוֹל וְהַנּוֹרָא

Chapter/Verse: Daniel 9:4
Hebrew: אֲדֹנָי הָאֵל הַגָּדוֹל וְהַנּוֹרָא
Transliteration: Ah-doe-nigh ha-El ha-Gah-dol veh-ha No-rah
Translation: Lord the Great and Dreadful (Awesome) God

Practice writing, saying Ah-doe-nigh ha-El ha-Gah-dol veh-ha No-rah.

NAME	SOUND		LETTER
Aleph	Silent		א
	ah		אֱ
Dalet	d		ד
Cholem	doe		דֹ
Nun	n		נ
Yud	y		י
	nigh		נָי
Hey	h		ה
	ha		הָ
Aleph	Silent		א
Lamed	l		ל
	El		אֵל

Hey	h		ה
	ha		הַ
Gimel	g		ג
	Gah		גָּ
Dalet	d		ד
Cholem Vav	oh		וֹ
Lamed	l		ל
	dohl		דוֹל
Vav	v		ו
	veh		וְ
Hey	h		ה
	ha		הַ
Nun	n		נ
Cholem	No		נוֹ
Resh	r		ר
Hey	h		ה
	rah		רָא

Ah-doe-nigh ha-El ha-Gah-dol veh-ha No-rah

אֲדֹנָי הָאֵל הַגָּדוֹל וְהַנּוֹרָא ....

Ah-doe-nigh ha-El ha-Gah-dol veh-ha No-rah

אֲדֹנָי הָאֵל הַגָּדוֹל וְהַנּוֹרָא ....

Chapter/Verse:	Daniel 9:4
Hebrew:	**אֲדֹנָי הָאֵל הַגָּדוֹל וְהַנּוֹרָא**
Transliteration:	Ah-doe-nigh ha-El ha-Gah-dol veh-ha No-rah
Translation:	Lord the Great and Dreadful (Awesome) God

This Chapter: Practice writing in Hebrew and saying aloud the Hebrew Title often. You can also make notes, list questions to research, etc.

Lord the Great and Dreadful (Awesome) God

אֲדֹנָי הָאֵל הַגָּדוֹל וְהַנּוֹרָא ....

_____

_____

_____

_____

_____

_____

_____

_____

Reflections

At this point in your study, consider taking time to reflect and think about why you have chosen to complete this *Simply Ev'reet Workbook Primer.* What goals did you set? Have they been met? Have your studies so far affected you in any way? From memory, what Names are you able to write in Hebrew? What other comments do you have? Date and list your reflections before continuing your studies.

Date: _____

_____

_____

_____

_____

_____

_____

_____

_____

_____

_____

_____

_____

Ah-doe-nigh Eh-lo-hey Ah-voh-tay-new ...... יְיָ אֱלֹהֵי אֲבוֹתֵינוּ

Chapter/Verse: Ezra 7:27
Hebrew: יְיָ אֱלֹהֵי אֲבוֹתֵינוּ
Transliteration: Ah-doe-nigh Eh-lo-hey Ah-voh-tay-new
Translation: LORD God of our Fathers

Practice writing, saying Ah-doe-nigh Eh-lo-hey Ah-voh-tay-new.

NAME	SOUND		LETTER
	Ah-doe-nigh		יְיָ
Aleph	Silent		א
	eh		אֶ
Lamed	l		ל
Cholem	lo		ל
Hey	h		ה
Yud	y		י
	hey		הֵי
Aleph	Silent		א
	Ah		אֲ
Vet	v		ב
Cholem Vav	oh		ו
	voh		בוֹ
Tav	t		ת
Yud	y		י
	tay		תֵי
Nun	n		נ
Shureq	new		נוּ

Ah-doe-nigh Eh-lo-hey Ah-voh-tay-new .... יְיָ אֱלֹהֵי אֲבוֹתֵינוּ

Ah-doe-nigh Eh-lo-hey Ah-voh-tay-new ...... יְיָ אֱלֹהֵי אֲבוֹתֵינוּ

Chapter/Verse:	Ezra 7:27
Hebrew:	**יְיָ אֱלֹהֵי אֲבוֹתֵינוּ**
Transliteration:	**Ah-doe-nigh Eh-lo-hey Ah-voh-tay-new**
Translation:	**LORD God of our Fathers**

This Chapter: Practice writing in Hebrew and saying aloud the Hebrew Title often. You can also make notes, list questions to research, etc.

LORD God of our Fathers .... יְיָ אֱלֹהֵי אֲבוֹתֵינוּ

_____

_____

_____

_____

_____

_____

_____

_____

_____

_____

_____

Eh-lo-hah Slee-khot .... אֱלוֹהַ סְלִיחוֹת

Chapter/Verse: Nehemiah 9:17
Hebrew: אֱלוֹהַ סְלִיחוֹת
Transliteration: Eh-lo-hah Slee-khot
Translation: God of Forgiveness

Practice writing, saying Eh-lo-hah Slee-khot.

NAME	SOUND		LETTER
Aleph	Silent		א
	Eh		אֱ
Lamed	l		ל
Cholem Vav	oh		וֹ
	lo		לוֹ
Hey	h		ה
	hah		הַ
Samekh	s		ס
Lamed	l		ל
Yud	y		י
	Slee		סְלִי
Chet	kh		ח
Tav	t		ת
	khot		חוֹת

Eh-lo-hah Slee-khot .... אֱלוֹהַ סְלִיחוֹת

Eh-lo-hah Slee-khot .... אֱלוֹהַ סְלִיחוֹת

Chapter/Verse: Nehemiah 9:17
Hebrew: אֱלוֹהַ סְלִיחוֹת
Transliteration: Eh-lo-hah Slee-khot
Translation: God of Forgiveness

This Chapter: Practice writing in Hebrew and saying aloud the Hebrew Title often. You can also make notes, list questions to research, etc.

God of Forgiveness .... אֱלוֹהַ סְלִיחוֹת

Ah-doe-nigh Eh-lo-heh-kha .... יְיָ אֱלֹהֶיךָ

Chapter/Verse: I Chronicles 22:12
Hebrew: יְיָ אֱלֹהֶיךָ
Transliteration: Ah-doe-nigh Eh-lo-heh-kha
Translation: LORD your God (MS/MP)

Practice writing, saying Ah-doe-nigh Eh-lo-heh-kha.

NAME	SOUND		LETTER
	Ah-doe-nigh		יְיָ
Aleph	Silent		א
	Eh		אֱ
Lamed	l		ל
Cholem	lo		לֹ
Hey	h		ה
Yud	y		י
	heh		הֶי
Final Kaf	k		ךָ
	kha		ךָ

Ah-doe-nigh Eh-lo-heh-kha .... יְיָ אֱלֹהֶיךָ

Ah-doe-nigh Eh-lo-heh-kha .... יְיָ אֱלֹהֶיךָ

Chapter/Verse: I Chronicles 22:12
Hebrew: יְיָ אֱלֹהֶיךָ
Transliteration: Ah-doe-nigh Eh-lo-heh-kha
Translation: LORD your God (MS/MP)

This Chapter: Practice writing in Hebrew and saying aloud the Hebrew Title often. You can also make notes, list questions to research, etc.

LORD your God (MS/MP) .... יְיָ אֱלֹהֶיךָ

_____
_____
_____
_____
_____
_____
_____
_____
_____
_____

Ah-doe-nigh Eh-lo-hey-khem .... יְיָ אֱלֹהֵיכֶם

Chapter/Verse: I Chronicles 22:18
Hebrew: יְיָ אֱלֹהֵיכֶם
Transliteration: Ah-doe-nigh Eh-lo-hey-khem
Translation: LORD your God (MP)

Practice writing, saying Ah-doe-nigh Eh-lo-hey-khem.

NAME	SOUND		LETTER
	Ah-doe-nigh		יְיָ
Aleph	Silent		א
	Eh		אֱ
Lamed	l		ל
Cholem	lo		לֹ
Hey	h		ה
Yud	y		י
	hey		הֵי
Kaf	k		כ
Final Mem	m		ם
	khem		כֶם

Ah-doe-nigh Eh-lo-hey-khem .... יְיָ אֱלֹהֵיכֶם

Ah-doe-nigh Eh-lo-hey-khem .... יְיָ אֱלֹהֵיכֶם

Chapter/Verse: I Chronicles 22:18
Hebrew: יְיָ אֱלֹהֵיכֶם
Transliteration: Ah-doe-nigh Eh-lo-hey-khem
Translation: LORD your God (MP)

This Chapter: Practice writing in Hebrew and saying aloud the Hebrew Title often. You can also make notes, list questions to research, etc.

LORD your God .... יְיָ אֱלֹהֵיכֶם

_____

_____

_____

_____

_____

_____

_____

_____

_____

_____

Roo-akh Eh-lo-heem .... רוּחַ אֱלֹהִים

Chapter/Verse: II Chronicles 15:1
Hebrew: רוּחַ אֱלֹהִים
Transliteration: Roo-akh Eh-lo-heem
Translation: Spirit of God

Practice writing, saying Roo-akh Eh-lo-heem.

NAME	SOUND		LETTER
Resh	r		ר
	Roo		רוּ
Chet	khet		ח
	akh		חַ
Aleph	Silent		א
	Eh		אֶ
Lamed	l		ל
Cholem	lo		לֹ
Hey	h		ה
Yud	y		י
Final Mem	m		ם
	heem		הִים

Roo-akh Eh-lo-heem .... רוּחַ אֱלֹהִים

Roo-akh Eh-lo-heem .... רוּחַ אֱלֹהִים

Chapter/Verse: II Chronicles 15:1
Hebrew: רוּחַ אֱלֹהִים
Transliteration: Roo-akh Eh-lo-heem
Translation: Spirit of God

This Chapter: Practice writing in Hebrew and saying aloud the Hebrew Title often. You can also make notes, list questions to research, etc.

Spirit of God .... רוּחַ אֱלֹהִים

_____
_____
_____
_____
_____
_____
_____
_____
_____
_____

Reflections

At this point in your study, consider taking time to reflect and think about why you have chosen to complete this *Simply Ev'reet Workbook Primer*. What goals did you set? Have they been met? Have your studies so far affected you in any way? From memory, what Names are you able to write in Hebrew? What other comments do you have? Date and list your reflections before continuing your studies.

Date: _____

_____
_____
_____
_____
_____
_____
_____
_____
_____
_____
_____
_____
_____

SECTION II

Sh-mah
V-ah-hav-tah

Sh-mah V-ah-hav-tah .... שְׁמַע וְאָהַבְתָ

The purposes of Section II are to reinforce and apply Biblical Hebrew learning through the study of Deuteronomy 6:4-9 and to learn selected information about Jewish People and the specific instructions to them from the God of Israel.

Deuteronomy 6:4-9 is a directive in the *Tanakh* to the Jewish People from the God of Israel that includes commandments, covenants, decrees and promises.

Reinforce your Biblical Hebrew reading, saying and writing selected portions of the **Sh-ma V-ah-hav-tah. Sh-ma translates to "hear and/or obey." V-ah-hav-tah translates to "and you shall love."**

Jewish people are direct descendants of the first Hebrew and the Father of the Jews—Abraham whose wife was Sarah. The Jewish people are descended from their son of promise, Isaac and then Isaac's son Jacob and his 12 sons--the 12 tribes. God made a special covenant with this people through Abraham and again at Sinai, where God gave His Torah, the Books of Instruction. In his time, Abraham and his people were the only ones who worshiped one God. The teachings, High Holy Day observances, celebrations, directives, covenants, and so forth, all are found in The *Tanakh* (Hebrew Bible--Torah, Prophets and Writings).

Jewish people for thousands of years, however imperfectly, have followed the commandments given directly from the God of Israel. I have found that many questions I had about Jewish people and their lifestyles were answered in the *Tanakh*.

Gentile people is a term for all other people groups.

The Sh-ma V-ah-hav-tah, selected portions of the Ah-me-dah, and the selected Scriptures from the *Tanakh*, have been essential to my learning. They are included in this Workbook Primer to reinforce your understanding of *Simply Ev'reet* and improve your knowledge of the people from whom this language originated. My hope is that this information will sort out misconceptions and help you enjoy an interesting, different approach to learning and understanding as you study Biblical Hebrew and several characteristics of Jewish Culture.

Sh-mah V-ah-hav-tah Deuteronomy 6:4-6

Reinforce your Biblical Hebrew reading, saying and writing the following verses from the *Tanakh*. Use your Hebrew/English *Tanakh*. Select words or phrases from Deuteronomy 6:4-9 and practice writing them in Hebrew. Learn and memorize verses 4 and 5 and write them in Hebrew. Select other words from verses 6-9 to learn and write in Hebrew.

Deuteronomy 6:4

Deuteronomy 6:5

Deuteronomy 6:6

Sh-mah V-ah-hav-tah Deuteronomy 6:7-9

Reinforce your Biblical Hebrew reading, saying and writing the following verses from the *Tanakh*. Use your Hebrew/English *Tanakh*. Select words or phrases from Deuteronomy 6:4-9 and practice writing them in Hebrew. Learn and memorize verses 4 and 5 and write them in Hebrew. Select other words from verses 6-9 to learn and write in Hebrew.

Deuteronomy 6:7

_____

_____

_____

Deuteronomy 6:8

_____

_____

_____

Deuteronomy 6:9

_____

_____

_____

SECTION III

God of Israel, The Jewish People, Land of Promise

God of Israel, The Jewish People, The Land of Promise

Commandments, covenants, decrees and promises, found in the *Tanakh*, given to the Jewish People from the God of Israel. Use your Hebrew/English *Tanakh*. Select words or phrases from the following Scriptures, learn and write in Hebrew.

Genesis 12:1-3

Genesis 12:67

Genesis 13:14-15

Genesis 15:18-21

Genesis 17:7-8

God of Israel, The Jewish People, The Land of Promise

Commandments, covenants, decrees and promises, found in the *Tanakh*, given to the Jewish People from the God of Israel. Use your Hebrew/English *Tanakh*. Select words or phrases from the following Scriptures, learn and write in Hebrew.

Genesis 35:12

Numbers 34:1-2

Deuteronomy 11:10-12

Ezekiel 30:5-6

Psalms 122:3-7

Reflections

At this point in your study, consider taking time to reflect and think about why you have chosen to complete this *Simply Ev'reet Workbook Primer*. What goals did you set? Have they been met? Have your studies so far affected you in any way? From memory, what Names are you able to write in Hebrew? What other comments do you have? Date and list your reflections before continuing your studies.

Date: _____

_____

_____

_____

_____

_____

_____

_____

_____

_____

_____

_____

_____

_____

SECTION IV

Ah-me-dah

Reflections

At this point in your study, consider taking time to reflect and think about why you have chosen to complete this *Simply Ev'reet Workbook Primer*. What goals did you set? Have they been met? Have your studies so far affected you in any way? From memory, what Names are you able to write in Hebrew? What other comments do you have? Date and list your reflections before continuing your studies.

Date: _____

_____

_____

_____

_____

_____

_____

_____

_____

_____

_____

_____

_____

_____

Ah-me-dah עֲמִדָה The Standing Prayer

Reinforce your Biblical Hebrew reading, saying and writing selections from the Ah-me-dah Use your English/Hebrew *Tanakh*. The Ah-me-dah (one of the two most important prayers in Judaism) is called the standing prayer from the root עמד which translates to "stand."

Psalms 51:17

Numbers 10:35

Proverbs 3:17-18

Lamentations 5:21

Reflections

At this point in your study, consider taking time to reflect and think about why you have chosen to complete this *Simply Ev'reet Workbook Primer*. What goals did you set? Have they been met? Have your studies so far affected you in any way? From memory, what Names are you able to write in Hebrew? What other comments do you have? Date and list your reflections before continuing your studies.

Date: _____

SECTION V
Additional Names of God

Additional Names of God

Genesis

Chapter/Verse

Exodus

Chapter/Verse

Leviticus

Chapter/Verse

Numbers

Chapter/Verse

Deuteronomy

Chapter/Verse

Additional Names of God

Joshua

Chapter/Verse

_____

_____

Judges

Chapter/Verse

_____

_____

I Samuel

Chapter/Verse

_____

_____

II Samuel

Chapter/Verse

_____

_____

I Kings

Chapter/Verse

_____

_____

Additional Names of God

II Kings
Chapter/Verse

Isaiah
Chapter/Verse

Jeremiah
Chapter/Verse

Ezekiel
Chapter/Verse

Hosea
Chapter/Verse

Additional Names of God

Joel

Chapter/Verse

_____

_____

Amos

Chapter/Verse

_____

_____

Obadiah

Chapter/Verse

_____

_____

Jonah

Chapter/Verse

_____

_____

Micah

Chapter/Verse

_____

_____

Additional Names of God

Nahum

Chapter/Verse

___

___

Habakkuk

Chapter/Verse

___

___

Zephaniah

Chapter/Verse

___

___

Haggai

Chapter/Verse

___

___

Zechariah

Chapter/Verse

___

___

Additional Names of God

Malachi

Chapter/Verse

_____

_____

_____

Psalms

Chapter/Verse

_____

_____

_____

Proverbs

Chapter/Verse

_____

_____

_____

Job

Chapter/Verse

_____

_____

_____

Song of Songs

Chapter/Verse

_____

_____

_____

Additional Names of God

Ruth

Chapter/Verse

_____

_____

Lamentations

Chapter/Verse

_____

_____

Ecclesiastes

Chapter/Verse

_____

_____

Esther

Chapter/Verse

_____

_____

Daniel

Chapter/Verse

_____

_____

Additional Names of God

Ezra

Chapter/Verse

_____

_____

Nehemiah

Chapter/Verse

_____

_____

I Chronicles

Chapter/Verse

_____

_____

II Chronicles

Chapter/Verse

_____

_____

Other Information

_____

_____

Reflections

At this point in your study, consider taking time to reflect and think about why you have chosen to complete this *Simply Ev'reet Workbook Primer*. What goals did you set? Have they been met? Have your studies so far affected you in any way? From memory, what Names are you able to write in Hebrew? What other comments do you have? Date and list your reflections before continuing your studies.

Date: _____

SECTION VI
Concluding Reflections

Reflections

Now that you have completed your personal Workbook Primer Reference Text, assess your progress. Why did you choose to complete this *Simply Ev'reet Workbook Primer*? Did you meet all of your goals? Why or why not? How have your studies affected you? Are you now comfortable writing in Hebrew selected Names and selections from verses in the *Tanakh*? What other comments do you have? Take some time regularly to date and list your reflections.

Date: _____

_____

_____

_____

_____

_____

_____

_____

_____

_____

_____

_____

_____

Reflections

Date: _____

Reflections

Date: _____

Reflections

Date: _____

Reflections

Date: _____